One of Fannin's Men

A Survivor at Goliad

One of Fannin's Men

A SURVIVOR AT GOLIAD

ISABEL R. MARVIN

Hendrick-Long Publishing Co.

DALLAS, TEXAS 75225

Library-of-Congress Cataloging-in-Publication Data
Marvin, Isabel R.
    One of Fannin's men : a survivor at Goliad / Isabel R. Marvin.
        p.   cm.
    Includes bibliographical references (p. 89).
    ISBN 1-885777-06-X (alk. paper)
    1. Goliad Massacre, Goliad, Tex., 1836—Juvenile literature.
    2. Fannin, James Walker, 1804?-1836—Juvenile literature.
    I. Title.
    F394.G64M37   1997
    976.4'123—dc21

                                                    97-11719
                                                       CIP
                                                        AC
            ISBN (hc) 1-885777-06-X (alk. paper)
            ISBN (sc) 1-885777-19-1 (alk. paper)

Illustrations: page 9 Texas Highway Department; pages 13, 33, 52, 66
Hendrick-Long collection; page 42 Archives Division, Texas State Library,
Austin, #68-2307 The Institute of Texan Cultures, San Antonio; page 75
collection of the author.

Cover and Interior Design:
Jared C. Wilson

Hendrick-Long Publishing Company
Dallas, Texas 75225-1123

Table of Contents

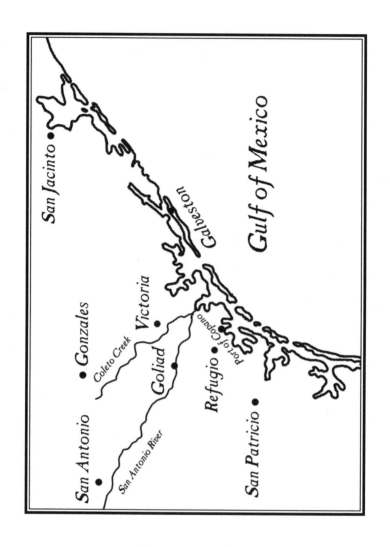

Dedication

This book is dedicated to the Wingate family who so kindly gave me access to their genealogical records charting the life of Edward Taylor Wingate, survivor of the Goliad Massacre. Through newspaper articles, family Bibles, personal records, and census reports, they have documented Edward's life.

There was no record of the Mexican family who took Edward in and cared for him, so I have taken the liberty of inventing a grandfather and grandson to do the job.

All facts about the Goliad Massacre are as accurate as research can make them.

I offer my apologies and sympathy to my history teachers at Goliad who tried to teach me about La Bahía.

Chapter 1:
The Field Trip

Benny mentally groaned and put his head down on his folded arms on the desk top. History! I hate it, he thought, especially Texas history! His teacher droned on.

"Colonel Fannin and 330 of his men, called Texians then, were massacred on Palm Sunday, March 27, 1836. They had been captured by Mexican General José Urrea, under the orders of General Antonio López de Santa Ana. . . ."

Oh, no, Benny thought, I can't stand it. His right knee began jiggling, making his desk squeak as usual.

". . . and incarcerated in Presidio La Bahía, which the Texians had named Fort Defiance. That is where they had been staying before the Mexican Army captured them," Mr. Pruitt said, touching a pointer to the outline on the chalkboard. "As you know, La Bahía officially became Goliad, our town, in 1829."

Tell me about it! Benny thought. I am so sick of studying about that dumb jerk Colonel James W. Fannin.

According to what Benny had read, the colonel

1

had never been able to make up his mind to act, which had caused the massacre. It may also have caused the fall of the Alamo when Fannin did not go to help the Texians there. Without realizing it, this time he groaned aloud.

"Benito Cantú! Are you taking notes?" Mr. Pruitt slammed the pointer on his own desk. "You are rude and disrespectful!"

"Sorry, sir," Benny said with a yawn calculated to further anger his teacher, "but I'm sick of hearing about Fannin. Every kid who lives here in Goliad knows the story."

The teacher was almost speechless with anger. Benny's best friend Ray Thigpen gave him a look that said, What's the use? We're going to have to listen to it just the same.

It was true, though, Benny thought. Hadn't the entire town visited Presidio La Bahía on the outskirts of Goliad, the place where Fannin and his men had been imprisoned? And that stupid monument out there that was built over their graves? That is, if anyone knew for sure where they were buried. As for him, he was good and tired of it. Forget the Alamo! Forget Goliad! Why were he and his fellow students being constantly annoyed with this junk?

"Benny," Mr. Pruitt said slowly, "you can sit here with me after school and tell me why Texas seventh graders should not study their own history. Explain it if you can." He took a deep breath, obviously trying to calm down.

By now the other students were talking quietly among themselves. They naturally assumed that as long as the teacher's interest was centered on one student, they could do anything they wanted to without fear of being reprimanded. Benny figured they felt the same way he did about Goliad history, but he was the only one with guts enough to say it. Ray shook his head and pointed to the big notice on the bulletin board by the classroom door.

Field Trip to La Bahía
All students' fees to cover the cost of the buses and entrance to La Bahía have been paid by the efforts of the student council and seventh grade classes.
Remember to bring your permission slips!

Probably the entire seventh grade would go. After all, it did get them out of an afternoon of classes. Okay, Benny thought, I'll shut up. Anyway, I'd better be careful. I may be getting a "D" in here by now. He leaned back in his seat and avoided the teacher's eyes. After a short pause for emphasis, Mr. Pruitt continued.

"Under the terms of the surrender, Fannin and his men were supposed to lay down their arms and promise never to fight against the Mexican Army. They could return to their homes and families if they agreed to this."

Then why were they all shot? Benny wondered. What did they do to deserve that? But he didn't really care. He hated history, especially Texas history. He picked up his pencil so that he would at least appear to be taking notes.

He and Ray had ridden their bikes out to the monument many times. There was nothing much there—couple of old cannons, a set of steps, and a memorial that looked like the Washington Monument only much smaller. The list of names in front was a little scary. To think that 330 men had been shot and then later buried in one grave was not something he wanted to imagine—although what they had been reading in school said more than that had been killed. Some had escaped, like the doctors and a group of men who were captured when they weren't bearing arms. A few others had been saved in some way or another. The so-called Angel of Goliad, Señora Francisca de Alinéz—or Alavéz—had saved a number of them. She was the Mexican woman who had come to Goliad with Captain Telesforo Alavéz, although Mr. Pruitt had told them she may not have been the captain's wife.

Benny knew his great-great grandfather Mario Benito Cantú had lived somewhere out behind La Bahía at the time. He'd been told often enough! Maybe it would have been his *great-great-great-great* grandfather. It had all happened in 1836, and this was over 160 years later. He tried to figure it out, but who knew how long his ancestors had lived then?

What did he care? Anyway, if he kept forgetting his permission form, he wouldn't have to go.

As the bell rang, Mr. Pruitt reminded the students to bring their slips the next day. "All those who do not have a written permit from their parents will have to stay here all afternoon in study hall while we go."

Bummer. He supposed he'd have to ask his parents for permission. After all, it couldn't possibly be any more boring than study hall for two and a half hours straight!

After school he stopped by Mr. Pruitt's classroom, hoping the teacher had forgotten his detention.

"Ah, here you are," Mr. Pruitt said as he drew Benny in and pointed to a desk. "Sit there for fifteen minutes."

"But I'll miss my bus," Benny objected.

"You should have thought of that before you smarted off."

Mr. Pruitt returned to the front of the classroom and his own desk. He picked up a document and looked at it for a moment.

"Do you read Spanish, Benito?"

Benny thought about not answering. This had nothing to do with detention or his history outline. Finally he said, "Depends on what it is."

"This," Mr. Pruitt said, "is a copy of the surrender terms that Santa Ana signed when General Urrea captured Fannin and his men. It's probably very formal Spanish, maybe even legal terms. I doubt if you could read very much of it."

Benny felt challenged. "Let's see." He took the

paper from the teacher, laid it on his desk, and struggled with the text. Holding his finger under the words and muttering, he laboriously translated for almost ten minutes. Then he looked up in surprise.

"Where did you get this?"

"The Mexican government kept it as a matter of historical importance," the teacher explained. "I bought a copy at a history convention last year. Is it pretty much what you have in your notes about Fannin's surrender?"

"No!" Benny said. "Nothing like it. I'll try to read the postscript signed José Urrea." Then haltingly he read:

"*'Since when the white flag was raised by the enemy, I made it known to their officer that I could not grant any other terms than an unconditional surrender and they agreed to it. . . . [T]hose who subscribe the surrender have no rights to any other terms. . . .'*"

"But, this means—" he paused, struggling for words.

"That they had made an unconditional surrender and could be killed if their captors made that decision," Mr. Pruitt said and nodded. "Fannin and his men never had a chance of getting out alive."

Benny paged back through the outline that he actually had copied off the board that morning. For a few minutes he compared the two. "Two sets of surrender terms," he said, "one in Spanish and one in English."

The teacher smiled and said gently, "But you

don't care. You hate history—and especially Texas history."

Benny hardly knew what to say. He floundered for a few minutes, trying to explain. "It's just that we live here where it all happened, but it has never seemed real to me. I'm sorry, but I'm honestly sick of hearing about it." He peered at the teacher, his eyes pleading for understanding.

Mr. Pruitt glanced at the clock. "Time's up. See you tomorrow on the field trip unless you decide to forget your permission slip." He stood and smiled at Benny.

Benny collected his books and nodded at the teacher, then walked down the hall. Maybe he should simply forget his parents' written consent. Then he thought about the two-and-a-half-hour study hall. Naah, even a field trip to La Bahía couldn't be as bad as that.

Chapter 2:
The Massacre

As the parade of Goliad school buses rumbled down Highway 183 & 77A across the San Antonio River toward Presidio La Bahía, Benny sat in the last bus with Ray, enjoying the warm spring weather. At least they didn't have to stay in the classroom on a day like this, he thought.

From the highway, the students could view the entire Royal Presidio La Bahía, which was surrounded by high stone walls with a bastion, a reinforced watch tower, set at each corner of the enormous parade ground. Inside there was a chapel, the soldiers' quarters, and the *calabozo* or jail.

When the buses pulled up at the main entrance on the west side of the old fort, Mr. Pruitt stepped out of the first bus and walked down the sidewalk releasing the eager students. By the time he got to the last group, Benny had begun to feel resentful again.

The teacher stepped up into the doorway and held up his hand to prevent students from rushing out too fast.

"You know how to behave," he said. "Please follow the column of students into La Bahía. The Presidio was restored in 1966; the crumbling walls were repaired, using the same stone. It still looks much as it did in 1836 when the massacre occurred.

"Big deal," Benny muttered as he got off the bus. Unfortunately Mr. Pruitt was standing behind the open door with the bus driver and heard him.

The teacher grabbed his arm and pulled him out of line, then spoke to Benny's friend, "Ray, you keep going. This young man wants to be at the end of the

line with me." His mouth stern, he stood by Benny until all the students had left the bus. "There, that's where you belong." He indicated that Benny should fall in at the end.

Benny shrugged to show Mr. Pruitt he didn't care about being last and sauntered along behind his classmates. By the time he reached the door of La Bahía everyone, including Mr. Pruitt, had gone in. He turned to inspect the outdoors once more. Maybe he could just slip away. Would Mr. Pruitt notice he wasn't there?

As he gazed around at the mesquite and prickly pear, he sensed that the landscape was darkening. He looked at the sky. Where it had been sunny and bright a few seconds ago, it was now becoming gray and threatening. A fog rose from ground level, obscuring the low grasses. His arms felt cold, and he hugged himself against the chilly air.

Should have brought a sweater, he thought, but it had been so warm this morning when he left for school. He gazed at the Presidio directly in front of him. It looked different than it had a few minutes ago, which puzzled him.

The fog seemed to swell and envelop everything. He wondered if a norther were coming. Sometimes in Texas, the temperature dropped as much as 30 degrees when a norther blew in. As the mist swirled around him, he saw through the billowing clouds a familiar figure walking toward him beside an ox cart. He could not know this person, yet he did. He had never seen him before, but he knew him well. Was he going crazy? What in the world was happening to him? Where was he? Then gently, easily, he slipped into the world in which he found himself.

"Grandfather," Benito called softly. "Is that you?"

"Sí, Benito, and Paco is with me," the old man answered. The small dog began to wriggle in joy as he saw his young master. Benito leaned down to rub his back.

"I wonder how much firewood the kitchen will need today," his grandfather said. "Yesterday the translator Señor Spohn told me we would not have to gather as much from now on. We are lucky to have Spohn, you know, although I suspect he has been an informant for the Mexican Army. He is one of the few inside the fort who knows both Spanish and English."

Benito nodded. "Without him, we would never know what the officers wanted us to do."

His grandfather concluded, "If they do not need as much firewood, some of the people must be leaving the fort. Maybe the Mexican soldiers are going to allow the Texians to go home. Let us go inside and ask." He paused and looked down at his grandson. "If your grandmother were still alive, she would have something to say about my not taking you to church on Palm Sunday."

"We will go next Sunday, and it will be Easter," Benito said in an effort to ease the old man's conscience. "Besides, most of the villagers are gone now. Maybe there is no service."

Just inside the door, Señor Spohn stopped them. "Señor Cantú? The kitchen has enough firewood for a few days." he said in Spanish. "It would be best if you did not come into the Presidio today," and his hand gently urged the old man and the boy toward the door.

"Paco," Benito whispered, and grasped the little dog by the leather braided collar he had made for him. "Not today," he said, and headed him back to the door.

The boy was curious about the prisoners who thronged the halls of La Bahía. They were laughing and joking, in English because they were the Texian troops, as they called themselves. They appeared happier than they had been for days. Benito looked at the translator questioningly.

"They have various jobs today," Señor Spohn said hesitatingly. "Some must bring beef for the kitchen to prepare; some will fetch wood, and others are going to Copano, perhaps to leave by ship for their homes." He walked to the door with them. "You know," he said slowly, "none of this would be happening if Colonel Fannin had obeyed General Sam Houston's order to leave this fort, then blow it up. He and his men were supposed to retreat to Victoria."

"All of *what* would not be happening?" Benito asked.

"Never mind. We'll go now," the grandfather said politely, "since we are not needed here today. "Come, Benito. It's a good thing to see the prisoners so happy."

Both of them opened the door and went out. The grandfather spoke to the ox, and they followed the dim path out toward their home near La Bahía. When they neared their small sod house, the distant rumble of many guns filled the air. Benito turned suddenly toward the fort.

"*Abuelo,*" he said urgently, "did you hear that? It sounded like lots of guns firing, all at the same time!" Again the blasting of muskets was heard, this time from a different direction. And then another.

His grandfather stood, a puzzled look on his face. "At first I thought it came from the Bexar road, then I heard it on the Refugio road, and yet another

volley near the lower ford of the river. What do you suppose—?" He stopped suddenly and gripped the boy's arm. "Benito, hurry home with me. This is nothing you should see." His eyes filled with tears. "Spohn told me—but I could hardly believe him. Those poor young men! They were so happy. They thought they were going home."

Benito pulled away from his grandfather's

restraining hand. "What happened? What did the Mexican soldiers do to their prisoners? I heard shots!" He looked at the tears streaming down his grandfather's face. "Did they kill them?" he asked. "Let us go try to help them," and he tried to turn back.

"It is too late. What could we do? I am sorry my grandson has to know about this. It would be dangerous for us to return to La Bahía now. Perhaps we can slip through the brush tomorrow to see what happened. For now, we will stay inside where we are safe." Then the old man groaned. "I should have taken you to the Carlos Garcia Ranch when most of our neighbors left to go there. I stayed because of my cattle, but we would have been safe if we had gone. It is fifteen miles south of here."

"Safe?" Benito questioned. "Safe from what?"

"From the guns of the Mexican Army," his grandfather said softly. "Now hurry."

Chapter 3:
A Survivor

The next day as mourning doves cooed and burbled outside the house, Benito woke up. He lay quietly for a moment on his pallet. In the opposite corner was his grandfather's bed, empty. Taking care of the cattle, Benito realized, as usual. Then a feeling of depression and dread filled his mind.

Yesterday. What horrible thing had occurred? But he knew what it was. It could not be anything else. The Mexican soldiers had marched the Texians out and shot them all. The musket fire had sounded too soon after Benito and his grandfather left the Presidio to allow time for a battle.

Had the prisoners permitted this to happen to themselves without even a struggle? No man would wait to be killed. He would ask his grandfather for his opinion. Outside he heard someone settling onto the wooden bench, the place where his grandfather traditionally spent many long hours whittling small figures.

Benito rolled out of bed and pulled on the homespun breeches his grandmother had made for him the year before. A rope belt held them up, but he was presently at work on a woven leather belt to replace it.

He grabbed several tortillas, still warm and lying on a dish by the kitchen fire encircled by stones on the dirt floor of their house. Then he ran out the door to sit on the front porch almost at his grandfather's feet.

"Good morning, *abuelo*," Benito greeted him.

"Did you sleep well, *nieto*?"

"Yes." He hesitated. "But I had bad dreams."

His grandfather sighed heavily. "I, too, was troubled in my sleep, and I have been out on the Refugio road to see what the shooting was that we heard." He stopped and a muscle in his lean brown cheek worked for a few seconds. "It was what we feared."

"The Texians have been killed."

"Yes, I think three different groups were being marched somewhere by the Mexican soldiers and did not expect death."

"So they did not fight."

His grandfather shook his head. "That is the way it looked to me." He leaned forward and momentarily stopped whittling, holding his knife loosely in one hand, the wooden figure of a dog in the other. "I do not want you to go near that area for a time, Benito. It is a sight that will give you nightmares for the rest of your life."

Benito gazed at his grandfather for a long moment. He had always obeyed him and, indeed, could not remember having any other parent. Benito's parents had died in the cholera epidemic when he was quite young. But this—this was different.

"I think I must see it. I need to know it is finished. We have spent weeks in Fort Defiance carrying wood and water, and we know many prisoners by their faces. I need to see it."

His grandfather once again began to whittle. "I was afraid you would say that. If I were a boy, I would feel as you do. But give me time—time to get used to the idea."

But Benito knew no one could ever get used to such an idea. "What are you carving today?" he asked as a change of subject.

The old man held up the figure. "It is Paco. This way you will always remember him."

The wooden carving looked almost alive. The dog's erect ears and inquisitive nose were pert and lifelike. His tail, caught in the act of wagging, curled at the very end.

Benito smiled. "It *is* Paco! He looks as he does sometimes when he appears to be smiling! That is the best figure yet!" Then he looked around in surprise. "Where is he this morning?"

"I had to tie him up, otherwise—you know."

Yes, Benito knew the curious little dog would be sniffing around the dead soldiers if they let him loose.

They spent the rest of the morning doing ordinary chores like carrying firewood for the kitchen fire, bringing a bucket of water from the village well, and deciding what supplies they needed from the La Bahía market.

After they ate a small meal of tortillas and beans for lunch, they yoked Sancho, their huge white ox, to the cart, and both climbed into it. The high wheels of the ox cart seemed to roll in an ominous rhythm, carrying them toward the river. What would they see that would haunt them for the rest of their lives? The trip, always a slow one behind the plodding Sancho, seemed to take no time at all because they dreaded it so.

When they reached the river, they started across where they usually did, where it was only three feet deep. Benito glanced at the nearest bank where something appeared to be half submerged close to shore. Bubbles rippled from the bundle in the edge of the water, and small eddies circled it. He watched it silently for a few minutes, then wondered if he were imagining that he saw a hand come out of the water. It appeared to reach for a bush as he watched.

"Grandfather!" Benito whispered. "What is that?" and he pointed to the spot.

His grandfather stared toward the ripples. "It is—yes, it is—we must examine it."

Slowly Sancho pulled the cart along the river bank. When they reached the place, Grandfather got out of the cart.

"Stay there, *nieto*, while I investigate."

But Benito had no intention of waiting. He crawled out also and followed his grandfather quickly.

The animal, or whatever it was, remained still as

18

they approached it. Once they were close, they could see that it was the sodden hulk of a man! The bloody water surrounding the man told the sad story.

"Dead," Grandfather said tersely, "or nearly." He reached in and grasped the man's hands to pull him farther up the bank, looking around carefully first.

Benito helped drag the man out of the river. The soldier sprawled on his face at their feet looked dead. His skin was as white as death; his clothes indicated that he was one of the Texians. They had not dressed in uniform but in casual clothes, such as he wore. He looked about thirty years old. They could not tell if he was dark haired because his hair was so wet.

"Grandfather! His wound is still bleeding. I do not think he is dead yet."

Blood issued in a small stream from the Texian's right hip. His pants were blood soaked. Grandfather bent over the soldier.

"Help me turn him over," he urged.

Together they rolled the body over. Grandfather knelt and held his brown fingers on the man's wrist.

"A pulse," he said in wonder. "He can still be saved."

The Texian remained motionless on the ground. Then a slight groan issued from the dead-white lips of the soldier. It startled them. Even Sancho backed up a few paces as if to escape from the unearthly sound.

Grandfather hurried to the cart and led Sancho to the soldier. By mutual agreement but without a word, the boy and the old man half lifted, half dragged the man to the cart and settled him into it.

Grandfather said, "There is nothing we can do for his wound here. If we delay, the Mexican soldiers may come along. When we get him home, we will take a look."

Benito picked up a dirty ragged blanket from the floor of the cart and carefully laid it over the man, even covering the head. His grandfather nodded in approval. Then without discussing it, they abandoned their trip for supplies and turned homeward.

Was the soldier dead? Or was he being given another chance to live? They were not sure. They only knew they had to try to help him. They also knew there was no way to hurry Sancho. In the distant skies, flocks of buzzards hovered over the soldiers' bodies.

Benny pointed them out to his grandfather.

"*Sí, los zopilotes.* Outside of those buzzards, no one except us is interested in the Texians any more."

Chapter 4:
Will He Live?

The journey home seemed much longer than usual to Benito and his grandfather. At any moment they expected to see Mexican soldiers demanding to know what they were doing. If they were caught trying to save this man, no doubt they would be shot too. The soldier did not stir, and indeed, seemed lifeless.

Why are we bothering? Benito wondered. The wounded man will only die—if he is not dead yet. But he knew that part of being human meant one had to help one's fellowman. He would have to rely on his grandfather who might know how to take care of wounds.

When Sancho lumbered into the yard, Benito and Grandfather looked helplessly at each other.

"I could spread a clean cloth over my pallet," Benito said eagerly. "Then between us we can carry him inside. He may still be bleeding somewhere that we have not seen yet."

At a nod from his grandfather, Benito ran into the house and prepared a bed. When he returned, the two of them struggled for a long time to drag the wounded man inside. They were not strong enough to lift him completely clear of the ground nor had they been when they put him in the cart.

The soldier was not a big man, but he appeared young and strong. Finally with the perspiration running down their faces, they succeeded in getting him onto the pallet. The man neither moved nor opened his eyes. Grandfather knelt and felt his wrist for a pulse. Benito held his breath. What if he had died from being moved? Grandfather took his hand away and crossed himself. "With the Lord's help," he said fervently, "we will save him. He lives yet."

Benito smiled. "We can do it," he said hopefully. "We must do it. All those poor dead soldiers—" Tears came to his eyes.

"First," said his grandfather, "go to the well and bring more water. We will undress him and clean his wound. His survival may depend on whether the musket ball went clear through his hip or is still in there."

"Have you ever taken a ball out?" Benito asked anxiously.

"No," his grandfather admitted, "but I have watched it done several times."

Benito ran to carry water. He brought in more firewood, and they heated some of the water. His grandfather directed him to lay out their only extra pallet so that all three of them would have a bed. It had belonged to Grandmother Cantú until this year, and they kept it rolled up above the rafters.

"He will be here some time, I suppose,"

Grandfather said. "And we must be ready to hide him in case the Mexican soldiers come looking for any survivors."

Benito could not imagine a place anywhere within the one-room house where someone could be hidden. They would have to solve that problem when they came to it.

Carefully, they opened the man's shirt and managed to draw it off. Next they removed his trousers, but first they cut along the seam of the pants on the soldier's injured side.

"I will clean off the blood and hang them on a tree branch. We will mend them because he will want them later," Benito said, but his grandfather only shrugged. Perhaps he did not think the wounded man would ever need trousers again.

Gently they washed the soldier's body with clean rags. When they turned him over to wash his buttocks, both of them realized that there was no exit wound, merely a ragged hole in his right hip.

"Still in there," Grandfather said softly and shook his head.

After they had cleansed his wound and bandaged his hip with soft rags, they spread a light cover over him and did not attempt to dress him. The soldier had not moved or spoken during the ordeal. His breathing was so shallow that both Benito and his grandfather kept anxiously watching the slight movements of his chest.

"Dampen his lips with clean water,"

Grandfather directed. "He's probably very thirsty but obviously cannot drink on his own."

Benito hurried to obey, and throughout the day they watched the wounded man carefully for signs of life. As his hair dried, it appeared to be light brown. Benito brought Paco in at suppertime not only to feed the little dog but to get him used to the stranger. After sniffing curiously at the prone figure, Paco ate, drank water, then settled down next to the soldier as if on guard.

"Look, Grandfather! Even Paco wants to help!"

His grandfather smiled. "We need more help than Paco," he said. "Do you suppose the *curandera* went to the Carlos Ranch with the rest of the villagers? She would be able to tell us what to do for the fever he is sure to get."

"Would it be safe to tell her?" Benito worried.

"I think so. The people here want their independence from that devil Santa Ana almost as much as the Texians do. But she may not be here in La Bahía now."

"I will go to her house," Benito offered eagerly.

"Not now," Grandfather said. "It will be dark soon. Go tomorrow, but you must watch for Mexican soldiers on the way."

Very early the next morning as first light filtered through the front door, Benito was awakened by a sound, a groan from the soldier. He's alive! he thought in amazement. He rolled quickly out of his pallet and lit the pecan-oil lamp that hung on a peg on the wall.

Benito held the lamp over the soldier and stared down at him. The man's lips worked, but if he spoke, Benito did not understand the words. He's thirsty, the boy thought.

Then he set the lamp down near the man and filled the dipper half full of cool water. He knelt and lifted the man's head. When the water touched his lips, the soldier opened his mouth slightly. Benito poured a little into his mouth, and although much of it ran down his chin, the boy thought he swallowed a little bit.

Benito laid the soldier's head down and felt the man's face. Hot. No doubt he was beginning a fever, as Grandfather had said. He hated to awaken his grandfather to ask what he should do. He carried a pail of cool water close to the man and began to bathe him completely, dipping clean rags into the water. A sigh escaped the soldier's lips within a few minutes, and he appeared to relax. Perhaps he sleeps now, Benito decided, and after watching him a few minutes for more signs of life, he blew out the lamp and lay down again on his own pallet.

Surely it was good that he was thirsty. When it is light, I will go for the *curandera*, Benito decided.

Chapter 5:
The Curandera

As soon as Benito had eaten his breakfast the next morning, he asked if he could go look for the *curandera*. He and his grandfather studied the quiet, pale face of the wounded man.

I think he drank a little water in the night," Benito said hopefully. "Is that a good sign?"

"Yes, it is. I will stay here and take care of everything while you go for Celia. Do you know where she lives?"

Benito shuddered. "Everyone knows where she lives. But except for the one time I went there to get help for Grandmother, I have stayed away. The *curandera* is a witch, I think."

"No, she is a healer. Go now, but watch for the Mexican soldiers. I'll take care of the cattle and do the chores. Better not tell her what has happened until she gets here."

When Benito left his house, he walked into the nearby woods. He remembered that it was a long walk to the *curandera's* house, which was like a cave built into the hill. As he walked, from time to time shafts of sunlight slanted down between the tall live oaks. On the way, he paused beside several sod huts belonging to his neighbors, but all were deserted. She would be gone, too, he decided.

Far ahead of him, he thought he heard men pushing through the brush toward him. Could it be Mexican soldiers? He left the dim path and hid behind a huge tree. He heard a group of men as they passed within fifty yards of his hiding place. He froze into position and stayed where he was until he could no longer hear their voices or footsteps. Since nearly all of the villagers had left La Bahía, the soldiers—if that was who it was—would not expect to see anyone in the woods. As soon as birds' songs were all he could hear, he left the tree and went back to the trail.

Finally he came to a small clearing with an herb garden. Celia's, he was sure. And there was the front of her house. He could see only the porch and a chimney protruding almost magically from the hill. The front door opened into the hillside. Who but a witch would live in such a place!

He tiptoed onto the porch. His friend, Nacho, always said you could tell a witch by her nose, long and hooked, and her thick eyebrows. "And she always has a lump of some kind on her face," he had insisted.

"So do lots of old ladies," Benito had scoffed. He wished Ignacio and his family would come back from the Carlos Ranch. Now that all the prisoners had been—were gone—maybe the Mexican soldiers would leave. Perhaps they had already left. Then he and Nacho could swim in the river, and fish, and hunt, and all the other things they liked to do.

The *curandera's* door was fastened only with a small piece of wood on the outside, turned to hold the door shut. She must be gone. After he knocked several times, Benito called her name, softly at first, then louder.

"Celia? Ce—lia!"

No answer came nor did the door open. Finally he cautiously turned the wooden latch to free the door. It swung lazily open. He peered in, then took several steps inside without even thinking of what his grandfather would say about such a trespass. No fire smoldered in the fireplace. Several pots sat on the hearth, and various baskets and jars filled the ledges built into the walls beside the chimney. A strong smell of earth and odors from medicine and herbs saturated the small room, but it was not unpleasant. Celia was clearly not in residence.

"What are you doing?" a harsh voice demanded, and Benito turned around so quickly that he almost lost his balance.

Confronting him was a woman, neither old nor young, but terrifyingly different. A dirty cap crowned her dark, straggly hair. Her face and hands were much darker than Benito's. She looked almost Indian. She was so close that he could detect the various exotic scents on her person and clothes. She moved aside to allow him to walk by her and out the door, all the while staring suspiciously at his empty hands.

"I asked you what you were doing here," she

said again.

"Uh, looking for you," Benito stammered. "I am Benito Cantú, and my grandfather Mario sent me."

"You may call me *Señora*," she said sternly, "and not by my first name! And I know who you are."

Indeed, Benito thought, she knows who everyone in our village is and everything they are doing, and no one can ever find out who tells her!

But she would not know why he needed her. He was reasonably sure of that. Was it safe to tell her of the soldier? It must be. When had she ever gossiped about anyone? But his grandfather had said to wait until she came to their house.

"Can you come help us take care of a—a person who has been hurt?" he stammered. "My grandfather will pay you what he can."

She stood silently, smoking a short pipe until he had almost given up hearing an answer.

"Wait. I will fetch my basket." She entered the house, giving him a warning look. He did not dare follow her. Soon she emerged, placing a ragged black shawl over her shoulders and carrying a basket that he assumed held small packages of herbs and ointments.

Benito walked along beside the *curandera*, occasionally holding a branch out of her way. She neither looked at him nor spoke, and he hesitated to break the silence. What would she think when she saw the soldier? Would she report them to the Mexican Army in the Presidio? Somehow he could not imagine her doing that.

It was noon before they reached Benito's house. Grandfather heard their approach and opened the door before the two could enter.

"*Buenos días*," he greeted Celia.

She peered at him for a few seconds. "*Buenos días*, Mario, my old friend," she returned. "It is good you have the boy now that your wife is gone. Otherwise, you would be very lonely."

Courteously, he inclined his head. "That's true. Now I must explain why we need you."

"You have rescued one of the Texians, one of Fannin's men," she said calmly. "A soldier who did not die as the others did."

Benito caught his breath, and he and his grandfather exchanged glances.

"Yes," Mario said, "but how did you—? *No importa*. Come inside."

Celia went through the doorway, looked around the small house, and set down her basket. First she removed her shawl, then knelt by the injured soldier. After pulling off the cover, she inspected him front and back silently. She held her brown hand on the pulse in his throat, watched his chest rise and fall, then examined the hip wound from every angle. She probed for long minutes against the hip, evidently trying to tell where the ball might lie. Then she shook her head sternly.

"It is going to be impossible for me to get it out," she muttered. "Perhaps he can learn to live with it. Stranger things have happened. Where did you find him?" she asked curiously.

"In the river," Benito said.

"I suspect he was trying to escape, and they shot him as he swam. He is a lucky man to be still alive."

Finally she grunted and arose. "His hip is no doubt torn up inside. Who knows if he will ever be able to walk again." She looked around the room, especially at the rafters where various spices such as garlic hung. "I will make a poultice of *ajo* to draw out the poison; I see you have plenty there," she said. "The hip wound may take him," she warned. "He is already feverish."

Celia directed Mario to cook their string of garlic until the buds were soft.

"All of it?" Benito said in astonishment. "We will never get the smell out!"

"There is another smell you would have a hard time getting rid of also," she said sternly, "rotting flesh. And that is what you will have if you do not prepare the garlic. It smells good," she insisted.

After some of the garlic buds were cooked until they were softened, she mashed them and pressed them onto the hip wound, no longer bleeding now. She wrapped a loose, soft cloth around the stinking mixture to hold it on the wound. Then she gave them an ointment of comfrey root.

"Later, after you have removed and replaced the *ajo* poultice several times," she said, then grinned as she watched Benito wrinkle his nose, "apply this ointment on the wound."

31

"We will need a ton of garlic," Benito muttered.

"Perhaps," she said. "Then make a cool tea for him with plenty of lemon in it. It will help his fever."

"We have a lemon tree," Benito said helpfully.

"If," she continued as if he had not spoken, "you can find comfrey root growing nearby, mash it and place it directly on the wound. Comfrey is good to heal broken bones and bruises. The hip bone is possibly shattered. We will know more later." Then she added, "*If* he survives!"

Mario reached under his pallet to pull out a few coins. "I am sorry it is all I can give you."

She nodded graciously and took them. "The Texians are fighting for our freedom also from the tyrant Santa Ana. I hope I live long enough to see that dream come true."

Benito was surprised to realize that Celia felt as they did about Santa Ana. She sounded almost like a normal person!

The *curandera* paused at the door. "Benito, you do not have to worry about my telling the Mexican Army about this poor man," she reassured him. "But I honestly do not know how you are ever going to send him back to his family even if he lives. Someone will recognize him as one of the Texians and then what?"

No one had an answer to that problem.

General Antonio López de Santa Ana

Chapter 6:
Sharing Names

By nightfall, the house smelled strongly of garlic although it was difficult to tell if the poultice was doing any good. The soldier's white skin had become red with fever, and Benito took it upon himself to sponge him off every few hours. He did not know when he had carried that many buckets of water from the well. If there had been anyone at home in the village, someone would have asked why he needed so much water. Fortunately, most of the villagers were gone. He wondered why the *curandera* had not left with them. Perhaps the only peace she ever had was when they were not around.

Several times Mario held the soldier's head so that Benito could try to give him water. Both of them felt that a few drops were making their way down the man's throat, but they could not be sure.

After they ate their meal of tortillas and beans, Benito picked some lemons and made a cooling tea for the survivor. Just before Benito fell asleep, he noticed that the man's face was not as red.

"What do you think, Grandfather?"

Mario shook his head. "He seems better, but I

cannot say absolutely that he is. We will pray for him."

Again in the night, the soldier groaned loudly enough to awaken the boy. When he held the light over the man, Benito could see that his eyes were open slightly. Blue eyes! No one would think he was Mexican. Even if he could sit in the sun for days, he probably would not look as dark as Benito and his grandfather did. How would they ever got a chance to smuggle him as far as the nearest seaport to start him on his way home, wherever that was?

Benito set the lamp down and held a cup of the lemon tea to the wounded man's lips. There! He was actually trying to take a drink. His throat moved slightly as the liquid slid down.

"More!" Benito urged, and held the cup again to the pale lips. But the man had already fallen asleep.

The boy watched him for a while. Did he seem to be breathing more strongly? He felt the pale forehead. Cooler, definitely cooler.

When daylight woke Benito, he crawled to the soldier's pallet and pulled down the cover to see the garlic poultice. It had slipped out of place, so the first thing Benito did was to cook another batch of garlic and prepare a new covering for the poultice.

The opening where the ball had entered the hip was not quite as angry looking, or so he imagined.

"Lord," Benito whispered, "let him get well and go home. Let us save at least one poor soldier from this horrible fate."

Grandfather got up sniffing the air. "Do you have any idea what we smell like now? I doubt if that odor ever leaves."

"I think it is doing some good, though," Benito said. "Besides, I can no longer smell it."

After they cooked some mush and ate it, Benito went outside to look for the comfrey plant. He remembered that the plant had large, hairy green leaves, and he knew enough not to touch them with his bare hands. Wherever they brushed against his skin, it would itch. When he finally found the plant, he picked up a stick and dug up the black root. Then he put one sandaled foot on the leaves to separate them from the bottom of the herb.

Inside the root, he knew, was a thick, sticky substance that contained the real medicine. He carried it back to the house and sat on the floor of their tiny porch. He pounded the root over and over until it was quite battered and beginning to release its juices.

"Now," he said triumphantly to his grandfather, "tonight, we'll put this on his wound instead of the garlic poultice."

It was several days before the two of them could see any real change in the soldier. One morning very early, Benito woke up to see the man looking around the house with wonder in his face. Then he said something to Benito, but it was not Spanish, so the boy did not understand. It would have been English, of course; all the Texians in the fort had been from the United States. While the man was alert, Benito eagerly held the cup of lemon tea again to his lips, and wonder of wonders, he actually drank some and sighed in satisfaction!

Later after Grandfather was up, the wounded man began holding himself in such a way that they both knew he needed to urinate.

"It is a good sign!" Mario exclaimed, and brought him a jar. All three smiled as the young soldier succeeded in passing some water.

"Now if he can eat something," Benito said happily, "maybe he will recover!"

But the soldier fell asleep before they finished cooking their breakfast mush. It appeared to be a relaxed, more normal sleep, however.

They kept up the cool sponging of his body and cleansing of the wound, which now was draining.

"I think that is a good thing," Mario confided, "the way the wound is running a bit. I remember once having a terrible gash on my arm from the time the bull knocked me against the fence. Your grandmother said it was a good sign when it did this."

At suppertime, again they cooked beans and tortillas, and Mario mashed up the beans to try to feed the soldier. He was able to eat a few bites before laying his head down with a sigh. He shook his head when Benito tried again.

Then Benito had an idea. He pointed to himself, "Benito," he said. He indicated his grandfather, "Mario."

The soldier observed this. Then he touched his

own chest and spoke what sounded like two words.

Mario frowned. "What did he say?"

Benito shook his head and reached over to touch the man's chest to ask him to say it again. "*¿Qué dijo?*" he asked. He supposed that even if the man did not understand Spanish, he would at least know it was a question.

Again the soldier tapped himself and repeated the same phrase.

"Eduardo!" Benito exclaimed. "It sounded a little like Eduardo!"

The soldier smiled and relaxed against the pallet again. "Eduardo," he repeated clearly, although the name did not sound exactly as it had when he first said it.

All three were happy to learn each other's names, and from then on, the soldier responded to "Eduardo."

But, Benito thought, how in the world are we going to take him anywhere without getting caught? He knows no Spanish. We know no English. And where is his home? We truly have many problems ahead before this very ill man will recover enough to go home. If the Mexican soldiers make a search for survivors and find one, they will surely kill all of us!

Chapter 7:

Ignacio

Benito, Mario, and Eduardo settled into a kind of routine for the next few days. In the morning Mario cooked breakfast mush while Benito saw to Eduardo's needs. Soon Eduardo was able to wash himself although he still had not tried to walk. Each morning after breakfast, Mario went out to the large pen in back of the house to feed and water his stock while Benito carried firewood, made tortillas, and brought water in for the household.

Their quiet morning was invaded one day by a shout from outside. Eduardo was enormously startled, but Benito knew who it was. In fact, he had been waiting for him. He smiled reassuringly at the soldier and patted his own chest. He meant to imply that the caller was a friend of his. Then opening the door, he greeted his friend Ignacio. He had already decided to tell him all about the soldier because Ignacio was a true friend.

Before allowing him inside, Benito stepped out onto the porch and closed the door. His friend, who was also thirteen, looked puzzled and slightly alarmed. His large ears stood out from his head and his slightly turned up nose seemed to twitch with curiosity.

"What is wrong?" he asked.

Benito smiled. "It is only that you must keep our visitor a secret, Nacho, and I wanted to tell you before you met him."

"I can keep your secret, Benito," Ignacio assured him.

"I know. Have you seen what has taken place near the Presidio?"

Ignacio's smile faded. "The killings? Everyone has seen them. You must have smelled the bodies burning from here."

"They burned the bodies?" Benito felt sick. "I knew I smelled something, but we have been inside the house and cooking so much garlic—"

His friend looked puzzled. "Yes, I could smell that long before I got here. Why are you cooking garlic?"

"We saved one of the Texians on the day that they were killed, but he had been shot in the hip."

Ignacio's mouth dropped open in surprise. "How did you do that?" he said.

"He must have dived into the river, and some Mexican soldier shot him. He has a musket ball in his hip that we do not know how to get out. Celia told us to leave it in. You can meet him." Benito opened the door for Ignacio.

Eduardo was leaning on an elbow, anxiously craning toward the door. Benito smiled to show him everything was all right.

"Ignacio," he said, pointing to his friend. Then he indicated the wounded man. "Eduardo."

Ignacio smiled and gave a tiny wave, as did Eduardo. Ignacio was clearly awed to be in the presence of a wounded Texian.

After standing on one foot and then the other, Ignacio suggested, "We could go swimming in the river."

"As soon as Grandfather is through with his chores. Someone must stay with Eduardo at all times."

"Oh," Ignacio said, "in case the Mexican soldiers come here. If you take him out on the road, anything could happen, but they may not think to search our village."

"We know. Soon, we will have to get him as far as Copano, the seaport, so that he can go home to his family. That is how most of them came here."

"It will not be easy," Ignacio warned.

After Mario came into the house, the two friends pantomimed swimming strokes to the smiling Eduardo before leaving. When he understood, he nodded his head and pointed to himself.

On the way to the river with Paco running around and around them, Benito told Ignacio where they had found Eduardo.

"He had been swimming all right," Benito said, "swimming for his life."

"Lucky for him that you came along when you did," Ignacio commented. "Are you afraid of the Mexican soldiers? They would probably shoot both you and your grandfather without thinking twice."

Benito shrugged. "We had to take him in," he said. "You know."

Then the boys raced to see who could dive into the San Antonio River first. They played in the cool water for several hours, as they had many times. On the way back to Benito's house, they kept a sharp lookout for Mexican soldiers around the fort, but they saw no one on the road.

"Did you see the bodies of the Texians?" Ignacio asked almost casually.

The March to the Massacre Col. Andrew J. Houston

Benito winced. "No. Grandfather did not want me to."

"They are stacked in three different places," Ignacio said, "the Bexar road, near the Victoria road, and the one to Refugio. It looked like they had been split into three groups, then marched out to their deaths," he said matter-of-factly. "The Mexican soldiers shot them, then bayoneted them."

"I do not want to think about it," Benito said softly.

"Someone will have to bury them," Ignacio pointed out.

"Bury them? You mean after they burned the bodies nobody buried them!"

His friend shook his head. "No, and they stink, too."

Benito preferred to spend his thoughts and energy on their survivor rather than men for whom there was no hope.

He and his grandfather had come to the point where they had to get Eduardo onto his feet. Perhaps, however, the poor man would never be able to walk. But he must, he must.

The atmosphere in the house became more relaxed after Ignacio had been there. Letting in the outside world had made them all feel better. Also, Eduardo was clearly improving. After a week of the invalid's sitting on the pallet and leaning against the wall, Mario decided it was time to get him on his feet.

Consequently, one morning when they all three had time, Mario indicated to Eduardo that he was going to help him stand. Eduardo evidently understood and raised both hands to meet Mario's. Slowly, carefully, Mario lifted Eduardo to his feet. The soldier smiled as he rose—until he attempted the first step. Then suddenly, an expression of extreme pain crossed his face, and he collapsed, almost sending his partner to the floor.

Benito sprang to help lower him gently to the

pallet, praying Eduardo would not fall on the injured hip and render himself helpless once again. Both the boy and his grandfather eased their patient down slowly.

"It is going to take time," Mario said, quite out of breath. He patted Eduardo on the shoulder and said comforting words even though he knew the soldier could not understand them.

Eduardo smiled but perspiration streamed down his face. Then he reached his hands up to Mario's again. It was clear he intended to try his best to walk.

Again Mario lifted him. This time, although his face was pale and his skin glistened with the effort, Eduardo managed three faltering steps. Then he sagged toward the floor, and Mario and Benito lowered him gradually to the pallet again.

"*Bastante para hoy,*" Mario signed with his hands, "enough for today."

Eduardo nodded, breathing hard.

But it was a beginning. Each morning at about the same time, the two helped the soldier to stand. Each day Eduardo remained on his feet a little longer. Finally the time came when he made it all the way to the front door. Out of breath, he smiled at them and nodded. He placed an arm around their shoulders, and slowly they took him out to the front porch and eased him down on Mario's bench.

Gasping and breathing hard, Eduardo sat with his head leaning against the front wall of their house. He looked around and smiled. The hot April sun streamed down over him. He gazed at the mesquite, scrub oak trees, and the corner of the cattle pen and smiled.

"Since all he has seen is our four walls for more than two weeks," Benito told his grandfather, "it is no wonder this pleases him."

His grandfather agreed, then reached under the bench and brought out the gift he had been carving for several weeks. With a flourish, he presented it to Eduardo: a walking stick, a beautiful cane intricately carved with small animals, flowers, and plants.

The soldier looked delighted and surprised. Several times he said something to Mario that they thought must mean *gracias*. Mario was happy with the reception of his gift.

Eduardo took the stick and tried to rise again, but he was clearly exhausted by the trip to the porch.

Benito said, *"Mañana,"* hoping the soldier would understand he meant tomorrow. Eduardo nodded and relaxed on the bench for at least an hour, obviously enjoying the sunshine. But the grandfather and his grandson realized that the moment was rapidly approaching when he would be able to leave. After Eduardo had gone to sleep that night, they sat on the porch to talk about how to get him to Copano, the nearest seaport. They knew that many of the soldiers from the north had arrived by ship there. Few of the Texians were from nearby and none from the La Bahía area, according to Spohn, the translator.

"We will have to take him in the ox cart," Mario

said. "He is not strong enough for any other form of travel."

"I do not know exactly how far it is, but it will take us more than one day," Benito worried.

Mario nodded. "We will have to stop at least one night with your grandmother's sister Juanita," he said. "I do not like to impose on her, but I do not know how else to make the trip."

"But—" Benito objected, "what if she reports us to the Mexican soldiers?"

His grandfather stroked his chin. "You are right. She would delight in telling them. I have never liked Juanita. It caused Yolanda many problems because I did not like to visit her sister."

"So that is why we hardly ever went to see her while Grandmother was alive!"

Mario looked guilty but nodded. Then he said, "Now that we are actually thinking of going, Eduardo would be safer—and so would we—if we could disguise him so that no one knew who was with us."

"Let me think," Benito said, and he sat for a few minutes pondering the problem. Finally he said, "I have an idea. I have to look for something. We will talk about this again tomorrow."

And he had an idea, such a crazy idea that it kept him awake for quite a while. It was daring, insane, but it might just work. It all depended on whether or not he could find something in the house—something that he would wager was still there.

Chapter 8:
Mario's Wife

The next morning, Benito began looking around the house for something to disguise Eduardo for the dangerous trip. He removed everything from the various pegs on the walls and then returned all but a few items.

Eduardo watched him curiously. Benito wished for the hundredth time that he could talk to the soldier. It was so frustrating not to be able to tell him what they were planning.

When Mario came in from his chores, he said hesitantly to Benito, "Perhaps we could wait and take him over to the Presidio when other Texians return. If," he said hopefully, "Santa Ana's army moves on."

Benito had not thought of taking Eduardo back to the fort. He frowned. "He cannot fight any more with that ball in his hip. What would the Texians do with him if he failed to keep up on their marches? You and I know he can walk only a few paces without stopping to rest."

Grandfather nodded. "That is true. Somehow I feel responsible to start him safely on the way home. What is your idea?"

Benito smiled. He indicated to Eduardo that he should sit down and watch what they were doing. Then he paraded the clothes he had found on the pegs.

"Remember this, Grandfather? It was Grandmother's favorite dress. It looks big enough for Eduardo. What do you think?"

The dress was black, washed so many times that it was quite faded, but it was loose and shapeless and had long sleeves. Mario held it up for a few seconds.

"Yes, we can try it. But you intend to—?"

Benito nodded. "Eduardo will be your wife. We will cover his light hair with this *pañuelo*." Then he showed him the large handkerchief Yolanda had worn on her head. They both looked at the soldier to see if he was understanding anything they were doing. Then Benito held the dress up to Eduardo and indicated he should put it on.

The man stared at Benito for a few seconds and then laughed. He took the dress and slipped it over his head. There, it fit fine! Then he reached for the *pañuelo* and placing it over his head, tied it under his chin.

All three laughed at the ludicrous sight! Eduardo looked down at himself, then held up one foot and pointed to it to ask a question.

"Shoes! I never thought of that!" Benito peered around the room and frowned, thinking of what to do. "I remember that many of the Texians wore black brogans, like low boots, but he must have kicked his off in the river. He has not needed shoes until now. All he has done is walk around the house and out onto the porch."

Mario said, "I will weave him a pair of leather sandals such as I have made for us, Benito. It does not take long, but first I must measure his foot. I have had the strips all ready to make another pair for myself."

Benito was excited. He pointed to Mario's feet and tried to indicate to Eduardo that he would have the same kind of shoes soon. As usual he could not tell how much the soldier understood, but the man nodded.

Then Eduardo pulled off the dress and kerchief and asked what sounded like a question. Neither of them understood. Finally Benito exclaimed, "I suppose he wants to know where we are taking him dressed like that."

He turned to Eduardo. "Copano," he said. He attempted to describe a boat with his hands. "We go to Copano so that you can find a boat for home." Each time he said *Copano*, he emphasized it, probably hoping that the soldier would recognize the name of the place.

Eduardo seemed puzzled at first, but then he repeated Copano and nodded quickly.

"He must have heard of it before," Benito told Mario. "Many of these Texians came here by way of ship. It is the closest seaport to La Bahía, or *Goliad*, as they call our village now." He smiled because he knew his grandfather's reaction to that name.

"It is called La Bahía, as it always has been," Mario insisted.

"All right," Benito conceded. "I will call it La Bahía, too."

In the days following their decision to get the soldier on his way, Mario spent any free time making the sandals. At last, they were finished.

Eduardo tried them on and smiled. Still leaning on the walking stick Mario had given him, he limped proudly around the room a few times and seemed to be trying to express his gratitude.

"When will we go, Grandfather?" Benito asked. Now that they were ready, he wanted to start.

"Soon. Patience, little one. We must get some food together for our trip, and a few blankets, for we will sleep under the stars several nights. It is about fifteen leagues to Copano. I do not plan to stop at Juanita's unless we are in desperate need."

Benito grinned. He was so excited! They would get through to the seaport! Then somehow they would put Eduardo on a ship headed for home.

"He might know someone official in Copano," Mario suggested. "As soon as he understands what we are doing, he will try to help. I am sure he longs to go home. I know I would."

Mario packed coffee, beef jerky, some beans and tortillas, and a jar of water. Then he folded two thin blankets. Eduardo's mended trousers and loose shirt were the last items.

"There is not much room in an ox cart for supplies and three people," Mario pointed out. "Mine is a large one, but still—" Then he said, "Who will take care of our animals while we are gone?"

"Ignacio," Benito said, then ran to his friend's house. "Nacho, we need you," he said breathlessly, "to care for Grandfather's cattle while we're gone and to keep Paco here."

"Where are you going?" the startled Ignacio asked. Rarely had the boy and his grandfather gone farther than the market.

"I will tell you when we return," Benito said. "It would be better if you did not know right now. Then if someone asks, you truly cannot tell them."

Although Ignacio looked puzzled, he agreed to stay in their house while they were gone.

"Do not worry about anything," he said proudly. "I, Ignacio, will be in charge!"

Finally the big day arrived. Sancho and the ox cart waited near the door as Ignacio ran up on the porch early in the morning.

"Here I am," he called. Then before his amazed eyes, his friend and Mario walked through the door escorting a strange old lady out of the house. She leaned heavily on her cane as she got into the cart.

Her hair was completely covered with the old kerchief, and she wore large leather sandals with her black dress. Ignacio's eyes were wide, his mouth open. Then he recognized her and smiled.

"*Adiós, Señora Yolanda,*" he said cheerfully. "Good luck on your journey." He extended his hand to Eduardo in farewell.

The soldier shook his hand and entered the cart. When he had settled into the seat, Ignacio moved closer to him and brushed his hand across his own eyes several times, shutting them.

"His eyes are blue," he reminded Benito and Mario. "Better hope no one notices them."

Eduardo seemed to know what the problem was because he ducked his kerchiefed head and closed his

eyes while they stared at him.

Benito nodded. "I think he understands."

Mario said, "We have done the best we can do. Say a few prayers for us."

The cart moved slowly out of the yard as Paco whimpered at being left behind. Benito wondered what trouble lay ahead of them on the road to Copano.

Chapter 9:
Bandits!

The road to Copano was well traveled. Mario estimated the port to be about forty miles from La Bahía and maybe more. Sancho lumbered steadily along, one heavy hoof after the other. The wooden wheels of the cart set up a rhythm for Benito; they murmured "Copano, Copano," over and over as they rolled. Although Mario remembered being there once as a youngster, Benito had never seen the port. He wondered about the boats and the water. He was excited about seeing everything but sad when he realized Eduardo would leave them, probably forever.

The countryside was the usual mesquite, cacti, and occasional live oak trees. They had to take the main road because the ox cart would not travel on the shorter route generally used by men on horseback.

When they were about four hours into their journey, Benito noticed blue elderberries growing beside the trail and begged to stop to pick them.

"They are blue," Benito assured his grandfather. Mario had told him never to eat the red elderberries because they were poisonous.

They allowed Sancho to graze for about twenty

minutes while Benito collected berries in his hat and carried them to the others. Mario urged the soldier to walk around with his cane when they stopped.

"His leg must be stiffening up," he explained to Benito. "When he is an old man like me, he will have great pain in his hip—especially if he still has that ball in it." Eduardo limped in a wide circle around the cart and in a few minutes was walking a little better. He rubbed his leg and grimaced as he climbed back into the cart when they moved on.

"See," Benito insisted. "How could he keep up with the Texians as they marched? He is in pain now."

They rolled on, observing rabbits in the brush and occasionally, green parrots in the cottonwood trees. After the sun went down, Mario called a halt for the night. They built a small fire, heated the beans, and made coffee. Eduardo lay on his left, the uninjured side, clearly trying to rest his right hip. He propped himself on his elbow to eat his supper.

Benito went in search of water to refill their jug. They would need it in the morning. He found a tiny spring that showed signs of having been a favorite camping spot. Ashes from an earlier fire were there, and several flat rocks had been gathered into a circle as if travelers had sat to eat or talk.

He brought the filled jug back and said to Mario, "People have camped here before. What if someone stops while we are here?"

"Then we will be friendly," his grandfather said. "My old wife is too ill to be a cook for them, but I will offer them a drink of water at least." He smiled at Benito. "Do not borrow trouble, *nieto*. We are safe here. I think we should roll up all our food and Eduardo's clothes and put the bundle high in the fork of a tree. Some animal might be interested in the food. And we do not want anyone to know that Eduardo is not a woman."

They searched for the best hiding place for their few possessions and pushed them as high as possible. Just to be cautious, they covered most of the fire with dirt and spread their blankets close together near it. Benito and Mario slept on either side of Eduardo, and although it was a strange place, they all fell asleep easily.

In the middle of the night, Benito awoke to a firm pressure on his shoulder, the side closest to the soldier. A slight squeezing of the hand there told him he must keep still and lie quietly. On Eduardo's right, Mario must have felt a similar warning because in a brief second all three were wide awake.

Shadows passed between Benito and the night sky, and he realized someone else was in the clearing with them. Hardly breathing in his fear, he tried to see all around them without turning his head or sitting up.

As the hand continued to grip his shoulder, he knew it was Eduardo who had awakened and warned them. Moving around the three quiet forms on the blankets were at least three, perhaps four men. Their bulky forms passed back and forth near the little group.

Bandits! Looking for something to steal. What should he do? Suddenly a foot kicked Mario's shoes.

"Get up and give us your food. Be quick about it," a low, rough voice growled in Spanish.

Mario sat up rubbing his eyes, asking in a sleepy voice who wanted him and why.

Another kick and this time, Benito felt it. All three travelers sat up. Luckily Eduardo was still fully disguised.

Mario stood. The sky was beginning to lighten, and a few red coals in the fire glowed, also. He must have been able to see at least where the men were even though he might not have been able to discern their features.

"We have nothing," he said humbly. "We ate what little food we had. Our blankets are all we have with us. You may take them if you wish."

"We do not want your blankets, old man. Give us your money right now or we will shoot you."

Benito felt a cold trembling in his stomach. Had they gotten this far only to lose their lives to robbers?

"None of us has any money," Mario said quietly, and turned out his pockets to prove it although it was doubtful the men could see what he was doing. Benito tried not to look toward the tree where they had stuffed the bundle of possessions. It wasn't much, but if they saw the soldier's clothes, they might discover it was a disguise. Who knew where their sympathies lay? They could be Santa Ana's spies for all he knew.

Then they would kill Eduardo. He assumed they were not Texians because they were speaking Spanish.

"I have no money either," Benito told them in a whisper although he was almost afraid to speak.

Suddenly the old woman got to her knees and began crying loudly and wailing unintelligible sounds—neither Spanish nor English. In fact, it was not any language that Benito had ever heard. It seemed fright, pure and simple. She buried her head in Mario's middle and clutched him, crying out in her fear.

"*¡Cállate!* Shut up! Can you not keep her quiet?" one of the men demanded.

"She's ill and frightened. I am afraid my wife is not herself; I am sorry. Perhaps if you left us, I could silence her."

Grumbling and complaining, the men walked hurriedly away. Benito heard sounds from a nearby thicket as the bandits mounted horses and rode away. Within five minutes, the frightened group could hear nothing except their own excited breathing. Finally they began to relax.

Chuckling quietly, they shook hands with each other and straightened their blankets. Still laughing, but quietly, they stretched out again. The visit from the bandits had disturbed them, but they were bone tired. The sun awakened them much later.

"What a night!" Benito said. "Let us get back on the road."

Mario reached into the tree to salvage their food

and belongings, and after eating a little, on they went. They must have all felt relieved to be safe and alone, but what would the rest of the trip bring?

Chapter 10:
Yolanda's Ghost

The next day the trail seemed to stretch out longer and longer as Sancho lumbered on. Along about four in the afternoon, they came to a small roadway that crossed the Copano road. Mario stopped the ox at that point. Benito looked questioningly at his grandfather.

"Why are we stopping here? We should look for a spring before we halt for the night."

Mario frowned. "We are running out of food, and anyway, my conscience hurts me. I think we better go spend the night with your *Tía* Juanita. She lives down this road. First, though, we should have a good story to tell her."

"A good story? Oh, about where we are going and why."

"*Sí.* I think we will say that we are going to San Patricio, which is a different direction from Copano. It is southwest of here. Anything but the truth. I do not trust her."

Eduardo looked from one of them to the other in a puzzled way.

Benito nodded. "We must protect him," he

agreed. "If we have to leave suddenly, we do not want anyone following us."

Mario turned Sancho to the right onto the path to his sister-in-law's house. After about thirty minutes, they came upon a small settlement where the sod houses were not close together. Mario paced beside the ox, stopping him in front of one of the houses. "*Tía* Juanita?" Benito called out. And again. "Juanita?"

When the door opened to allow an old lady outside on the porch, she took one look at Eduardo and began to shriek. They had forgotten that the soldier was disguised in her sister's clothes. Neither Mario nor Benito had bargained for the tremendous shock their passenger gave Juanita. As his great aunt screamed, Benito turned to Eduardo and held his finger briefly in front of his lips as a warning.

The thin woman covered her eyes and continued to scream until Mario put his arm around her soothingly.

"It is not a ghost," he assured Juanita. "My friend Elena is wearing Yolanda's clothes. We forgot, uh, that you have not met her yet."

Finally she took her hands away from her face and looked closely at Eduardo.

"*¡Dios mío!*" she said weakly. "Are you trying to kill me, Mario? What are you doing here? And who on earth is this?"

"Uh, we are taking Elena to San Patricio," he said, "as a favor to Celia, who is her sister. We have

given her some of Yolanda's clothes because she has
so little. We have no use for them, of course. Also she
has—broken her hip. Do you remember Celia, our
curandera?" He smiled, which seemed to infuriate
her. "Did you think it was the ghost of your sister
Yolanda?"

She slapped his forearm. "Of course I did!
What did you think I would do? My sister wore that
dress for fifteen years." She peered closely at
Eduardo, whose kerchief was pulled down to his eyes,
that were almost closed.

"This is Elena Garcia," Benito said quickly.
"She is both deaf and dumb, but she is harmless. She
is going to live near San Patricio with another rela-
tive."

Juanita looked at the soldier suspiciously.
"Humph!" she grunted. They were not sure she was
convinced it was a woman, but perhaps she was too
polite to question them. "I am getting ready to eat.
Will you come inside?"

After taking Sancho to graze behind the house,
the three travelers sat down to a meal of *cabrito* stew.
They were hungry and had not had any meat for several days, so they ate all they could hold of the deli-
cious goat dish. Benito thought probably it had been
intended to last for several days. He noticed that
Juanita watched the soldier limp when he went out
back to the privy.

"Elena is the *curandera's* old sister," he said,
"and she is not well. At Christmas time she broke her

hip. She is also going blind. That is why her eyes look so funny," he improvised.

Juanita peered suspiciously at the old woman's face when she returned, but the kerchief was pulled low over the eyes. Night was approaching, and the room was dimly lit. She began putting away the remnants of the meal she had prepared. "I know all about leg pain," she grumbled. "Last year I broke my left ankle. I could have used some help," she complained to Mario.

"It is too bad I did not know," the old man said pleasantly. "Would you like Benito and me to chop some wood for you while we are here?"

"Yes," she said sternly. "You should be good for something. Where do you think you are going to sleep in this small house?"

"On this trip we have become used to sleeping outside," Mario insisted. "We do not mind."

"But what about—Elena?" Juanita asked.

"She would be afraid if she did not stay with us," Mario explained hastily. "Benito and I will cut a nice pile of kindling for you tomorrow early in the morning."

After the meal, the visitors, who now felt more like intruders, took their blankets out back near the meadow where Sancho was hobbled.

By the time it was completely dark, they were all three stretched out on their blankets. Then Benito noticed that his great aunt was no longer in her house. He could see her carrying a lantern and running through the trees toward a neighboring house.

"Grandfather?" he whispered to Mario. "*Tía* Juanita has gone to the house next door. Do you think she is suspicious?"

Mario sat up immediately. "She might be. We're trapped behind her house now. Let us get up and go down this small path until we find another crossroad and can return to the Copano road."

"In the dark?" Benito asked.

"Looks like we will have to," Mario said softly. He yoked Sancho again to the cart, and Benito helped Eduardo climb in. Mario walked beside Sancho to guide him. Fortunately it was a bright night, and with the light from the moon and some vague memory of Mario's, they rolled down the small road. Bushes and brambles alongside the path whipped them often. About twenty minutes later, they heard a great commotion behind them. People were thrashing around through the trees near the old aunt's house and calling to each other.

"Grandfather!" Benito whispered anxiously.

"Shhhh. We will keep going as long as we can. I do not think they can hear Sancho from there. Remember, they think we are going to San Patricio, so they will look first in that direction. It is a long way to San Patricio, so that should keep them busy for a while."

The little group continued down the trail. It was not possible to hurry the ox. From time to time, cloud shadows dimmed the bright face of the moon as the terrified travelers fled. They had gotten this far without being stopped. Why had they decided to go to Juanita's?

Chapter 11:
Copano

The rest of the journey was uneventful although they kept a sharp lookout for pursuers. By sundown two days later after a long and difficult trip, the ox cart rolled into the outskirts of Copano. On the way into the port, they passed a wagonload of women taking their wash out to a creek near the town. Mario pointed out that fresh water must be a problem there.

Mario piloted the cart all the way to the harbor. They hoped they could find a Texian who might be able to help Eduardo continue on his way home, wherever that was.

The harbor was a scene of great activity. Small boats plied between the wharf and two and three-masted schooners anchored about 300 yards out. Half a dozen buildings near the wharf looked like homes, and one long, low building by the water was clearly used as a storage shed for people who planned to come ashore to find a place to live. They probably left their goods and furniture temporarily in the storage building, Mario told Benito.

Among the people busily going about their

activities were a few in the same type of clothes
Eduardo had worn. Benito pointed them out to his
grandfather.

Mario directed Benito to a grassy area near the
water's edge. "Take Sancho over there, and let him
graze. I am sure he is hungry and tired of this travel-
ing."

Obediently Benito led the big white ox to an
area free of people and released him from his yoke.
Then Benito sat down to wait and enjoy the sights and
sounds of the port.

He watched curiously as Mario and Eduardo
disappeared into the front door of a small inn near the
waterfront. After about fifteen minutes, they emerged
with Eduardo dressed in his own dark pants and loose,
light shirt although without a hat. It had no doubt been

lost when he dived into the San Antonio River weeks ago.

Benito felt pride fill his throat. Eduardo was every inch a Texian, even in his casual clothes. Most of the Texians in the Presidio had not worn uniforms, but Benito was sure everyone could tell he was a soldier. He watched the two carefully as they walked along the wharf, clearly looking for someone to whom Eduardo could talk. A tall Texian, dressed in a similar fashion, stopped when Eduardo hailed him. Then the two not only shook hands but embraced each other. They talked excitedly as Mario stood by smiling. Then the three of them walked over to Benito.

The taller soldier greeted Benito in Spanish. His knowledge of the language was limited, but he was able to aid communication between the Cantús and Eduardo.

"My friend Edward Wingate," the man said, "thanks you for saving his life. Without you, he would have died."

Benito was glad to know Eduardo's full name. Both Mario and Benito smiled.

"He is very welcome," Mario said graciously. "Can you help him get home?"

"Yes," the soldier said and paused, glancing uncomfortably at Eduardo, "or I can help him get back to his regiment—what there is left of it."

Benito and his grandfather had wondered if Eduardo knew of the massacre. Evidently he did, from what his friend said. At any rate, Eduardo would not have tried to escape in such a dangerous way unless he had known they were all being killed.

Benito was anxious to get Eduardo started on his way home. "He cannot fight again! He has a musket ball in his hip. He should go home to his family."

Eduardo smiled when his friend translated Benito's concerns. Then he evidently explained his feelings to his friend. The other soldier shrugged.

"I'll help him do whatever it is that he wants to do. I'll take him to my colonel," he said. He spoke with Eduardo again briefly. "He wishes he had something to give you," the man said, "but he has nothing. He has some pay coming, so I will advance that and give you a little money."

Mario waved his hands to say no.

"It is not much," the soldier said, "but it will buy you a meal and a night at an inn. It is a long way back to La Bahía in an ox cart."

Benito and Mario looked at each other. They felt it would be gracious to accept the money, but both instinctively knew that no innkeeper would ever get it. They would be on their way as soon as Eduardo left them. Then they would sleep by the roadside as they had before. It would be a rare treat to have a little cash, though.

The soldier handed Mario the money.

"Thank you," Mario said and inclined his head. Then both of the Cantús shook hands vigorously with Eduardo. He reached down and hugged Benito, who held back tears with an effort. They yoked Sancho again and began driving back toward the road to La Bahía as Eduardo waved again and again with his cane. Soon Benito could no longer see him.

The boy felt curiously empty, as if he had lost something valuable. A friend, he thought, I have lost a friend that I will never see again in my life. He tried to stop the tears that insisted on rolling from his eyes.

Mario patted his grandson's knee. "It is a good thing that we did, *nieto*. It will be a wonderful memory for us. Eduardo is a good man."

"I know," Benito sobbed, "but I will miss him."

"I will, too," Mario agreed, "and I have a feeling he is not going to his home. He wants to fight again!"

"Maybe he cannot," Benito said, wiping his eyes with his arm.

"Oh, yes. He will improve in time. I think he is a dedicated soldier, and that is the life he wants."

Benito straightened up. "If it is what he wants, I hope he gets it."

The days of travel seemed endless. Benito got out and walked most of the time. He no longer enjoyed the motion of the ox cart. When they came within sight of their house at last, both of them cheered. It had been a difficult trip. Ignacio ran out the front door with Paco as they drove up.

"Everything is fine," he shouted. "I am a good landowner. I fed the cattle, and Paco and I played together. I am glad you are here finally, though."

Then he looked at Mario getting out of the cart as Paco bounced and capered around Benito's legs.

"Where is—did you leave Eduardo in Copano?"

"Yes," Benito said, "with other Texians. No doubt he will be fighting again—unless the Revolution is over."

"I suppose you heard the news!"

"News?" Benito asked.

"The Texians have beaten Santa Ana!" Ignacio said and grinned.

"What are you saying?" Mario placed his hand on the boy's shoulder. "Can this be true?"

Ignacio repeated it. "The Mexican Army outnumbered the Texians almost two to one at San Jacinto April 21, right after you left! A great day in history to remember. The Mexicans had about 1500 to 1600 soldiers, but the Texians captured Santa Ana and either killed or took all of his men prisoner!"

It was welcome news. Soon the Texians would take over Fort Defiance again. How Mario and Benito wished they could tell Eduardo! Benito wondered where he was—on his way home or looking for another regiment so that he could fight again.

Even so, they agreed that the Revolution probably was not at an end. The two boys decided to go to the river for a swim, and Mario, groaning, went behind the house to the cattle pen.

"That was too long a trip," he complained as they left the yard. "My old bones will never be the same. I have had too many saint's days!"

Chapter 12:
A Burial

The sun was high when Benito got up the next morning. He felt safer sleeping in his own house than on the road, and he was glad to be home. After he ate tortillas, he followed his grandfather around and helped with chores for part of the morning. He missed Eduardo. Taking care of the soldier had become their focus, and it was difficult to realize that their lives would be different now.

The news of San Jacinto was most welcome. Soon the Texians would take over Fort Defiance again. How Mario and Benito wished they could tell Eduardo! Benito wondered where he was.

Mario said, "I hope the Texian soldiers come soon. Someone needs to do something about—you know."

"Yes," Benito said, "the bodies."

As usual in the late spring, a number of Mario's cows began calving, and both of them were busy night and day. Benito had no time to mourn the loss of Eduardo. He realized now that Eduardo's safety had been on their minds every day.

By early June, the Texian forces returned. Once

again, the white flag with the blue star flew above Fort Defiance. Word went out that there was to be a mass burial.

On June 3, the newly arrived Texians under General Thomas Rusk, finally buried the massacred Texians' bones in one huge grave. Mario told Benito to stay home while he went to help that day. When he came home to supper, he looked sick. He washed his entire body several times, but he insisted he could not get the stench out of his nostrils. Benito had prepared supper, but Mario only gagged and when he sat down, he was unable to eat. It was best that Eduardo did not know how the bodies of his fellow Texians had been treated.

The next day Mario said, "Let us go over to the fort and see if we can work for the new group of Texians. We will see if anyone speaks Spanish and then ask for work."

Paco chased along beside them as they went. The day was beautiful, blue skies, hot sun, and tiny scudding clouds up high. Benito called the little dog back several times as he tried to explore too far.

Benito walked with his head down beside his grandfather. When they were near the fort, Benito tried to tell Mario how much he missed Eduardo.

"Do you think he will remember us? I know we will not forget him. By now, perhaps he is on the way home to his wife—if he has one. What a story he will have to tell her!" Then he realized he had outpaced his grandfather and turned to wait for him. But something strange was happening.

The day was darkening and the air becoming chilly. His grandfather seemed rather far behind him. In fact, he could hardly see the old man because of the ground fog billowing up around him. Benito had the odd impression of waking from a dream, of trying to remember where he was and what had just happened. For a moment, he knew he was at the door to La Bahía; then he seemed to forget his purpose in being there.

"Grandfather!" he called. "Hurry up!" But Mario and Paco were fading. Soon he could no longer see them. As he reached for the door to the Presidio, it suddenly burst open.

Hurrying out the door were Benny's classmates, running by him as they sped toward the Fannin Memorial only a few hundred yards away. His friend Ray Thigpen hurried to his side.

"Where've you been?" Ray asked. "I knew you had to wait until last to come in, but I never did see you inside the Presidio."

Benny stared at him. The strangest sensations ran through his mind and body. *Where had he been?*

"I was nowhere. Just right here," he said. "Is it time to go see the monument now?"

"Yeah, come on!" Ray ran hastily after the others, and Benny followed.

Several students tried straddling the two old

cannons sitting on either side of the main walk leading up to the monument steps. Mr. Pruitt immediately scattered them.

"The cannons were used by Colonel Fannin to defend Fort Defiance. Don't play on them. One night in February, 1936, one hundred years after the massacre, two men, using metal detectors, located these cannons. They had been buried inside the mission wall. The men removed them and took them away— all this without permission—but they were finally persuaded to return them."

The students ran up the steps to the Fannin Memorial. Horizontal granite panels covered with names was the base for the obelisk, an oblong pillar thirty-five feet in height. At the top of it was a stone sculpture of the Goddess of Justice holding a lone star aloft in her left hand as she knelt to lift the chained figure of a soldier.

Students began chanting the names loudly as they ran up the steps and back down. Ray and Benny climbed the stairs to look at the list of 330 names, Texians who had been massacred with Colonel Fannin. They had seen them many times, of course. Idly, Benny ran his eye over the names.

His glance fell upon a particular name on the right-hand side of the monument as they faced it. Edward Wingate. It seemed familiar. Why would one of these be a name he knew? He shivered.

"What'sa matter?" Ray asked. "Somebody walk across your grave?"

"Something like that," Benny muttered. He could think of no reason why he should know that name—or any other name on the wall.

"Let's go!" Ray urged. "The buses are here."

The seventh graders sped to find their buses, eventually getting into some kind of order to board.

After they sat down for the homeward ride, Ray said, "You feel sick or something, Benny?"

"No. Nothing like that."

"Got an easy day coming up tomorrow in history class," Ray said in satisfaction. "We're gonna discuss the field trip, then take our big test on Fannin the next day."

The buses drove back to the middle school and let the students off.

"See you tomorrow!" Ray called while Benny walked slowly into the school to his locker. He leaned his head against it for a few minutes, trying to remember what he had forgotten. It was a strange feeling.

Chapter 13:
A Little Dog

The next afternoon in history class, students were excited and interested in discussing the field trip. Many had additional questions after seeing La Bahía Museum. They had looked at displays in the large rooms inside the stone walls: sketches of the Texians as they might have appeared in 1836, weapons, musket balls, and old documents pertaining to that long ago fight in Fort Defiance. The early flags of Texas Independence stood in glass cases.

"We especially liked the flag that had that bloody arm and a sword on it," one student said.

The teacher laughed. "Trust you guys to like that one! The idea was that the Texians would rather cut off their right arms than lose their independence! But that isn't the one that flew over the fort when Fannin was there."

"No," Benny mumbled, "that one was white with a blue star on it."

Ray jerked his head around to stare at his friend.

In the back of the classroom, Olga Rivera raised her hand. "Mr. Pruitt, don't you think it's just awful that the commander of Fort Defiance—Colonel

Fannin—wouldn't ever do anything until it was too late? The massacre was really his fault!"

Mr. Pruitt listened carefully to her question. Benito raised his hand.

"Just a moment, Benito. I want to try to answer Olga's question first."

"But, sir, could I answer it?"

An amazed expression passed over the teacher's face. He dropped into the chair at his desk.

"By all means!" he said in a surprised tone.

Benny turned to look at Olga. The students became quiet. For Benny to volunteer anything in history class was a first. Ray looked at his friend with a puzzled frown.

"Olga," Benny began, "Fannin had nothing but bad choices to make. If he had taken his men and gone to the Alamo as Travis asked, he would have been caught in the same trap as the rest of those killed there. After all, the Mexican forces gathered at San Antonio numbered between 4000 and 6000 men. What could a few hundred Texian soldiers do—especially when Fannin and his troops had to walk 100 miles through rough country to get to the Alamo."

The expression on Mr. Pruitt's face was only admiration at that point.

Benny went on, "Both Travis and Fannin had been ordered by General Sam Houston to get out of their situations, blow up their forts—the Alamo and Fort Defiance—and retreat to Victoria. Neither one of them did that."

"Didn't Houston order Fannin to go to Travis's aid in the Alamo?" another student asked. "He disobeyed a direct order."

"Not really," Benny said before Mr. Pruitt could speak. "It may have looked that way then, but the truth is that he didn't receive the order in time. The Alamo fell on March 6, and Houston's request for Colonel Fannin, at Goliad, and Neill, commander at Gonzales, to help the Alamo didn't reach them until either March 13 or 14, way too late. Finally, Fannin and his men left La Bahía on March 19 in order to retreat to Victoria. They had no food or water, their wagons were broken down, and they were caught out in the open by superior Mexican forces. So they surrendered at Coleto Creek."

"How do you know all that?" Juan López asked without raising his hand.

"Juan—" Mr. Pruitt warned.

"I'm sorry, but how does Benny know so much about Fannin? Just this week he said he didn't want to hear any more about Fannin and the massacre."

"Yeah, yeah," several students agreed.

Mr. Pruitt looked at Benny. "Perhaps you can explain. Frankly, I'd like to hear the answer too."

Benny was embarrassed. "I don't know," he said slowly. "You know my great-great—maybe four greats—grandfather Mario Benito Cantú used to live in La Bahía, the village, I mean, not the fort. I suppose stories have been passed down in our family through the years. Also," he reminded the teacher, "you gave us the names of some extra books to find in the library. My dad collects books about it, too."

Then Benny added slowly and thoughtfully, "The way I look at this massacre thing is that it was a no-win situation, and Fannin's been the scapegoat ever since."

Mr. Pruitt nodded. "Yes," he said, "that's the way I see it."

The bell rang, and the students streamed into the hall.

"You feeling okay?" Ray asked anxiously as they hurried to their lockers.

"Sure," Benny said. "Why?"

"It's just that you don't act like the kid who hates history any more."

Benny shrugged. "That's true, but I don't know why. Come over tonight and we'll study for the test together. Maybe I can still save my history grade."

After school, the bus let Benny off as usual on the Berclair road. He slipped his backpack straps over his shoulders and trudged up the dusty roadway to his parents' ranch house. Jack, his big collie, ran to greet him, and they walked together to the front door.

"I'll be out as soon as I find something to eat," Benny promised the collie, who settled on the porch to wait. Usually he took Jack out to the barn and saddled his horse Rusty for a ride. Today Benny felt as if he had something he needed to do, but for the life of him, he couldn't remember what it was.

He raided the refrigerator, then went to his

father's study. As he ate a peanut butter sandwich and a peach, he looked over the titles of the many Texas books covering one wall of the room.

Why wouldn't I know about Colonel Fannin? he asked himself. My dad's been gathering books about that massacre and the Alamo all his life. Why would the teacher think I didn't know about it?

He knew the answer to that. He, himself, had made it quite clear that he didn't want to hear any more about the massacre. After he finished eating, he wiped off the desk and selected a few of the books to look at. Soon he was deeply involved in the old story of the massacre. He remembered his grandmother telling him about the dedication of the Fannin Memorial when she was in high school in 1938.

"No one really knew where the bones of the Texians were buried," she had said. "But they did find fragments of human bones underground in the spot where they decided to build the monument. Actually gophers dug some of them up. The bones had been burned, a good sign that those were fragments of the original massacre."

Benny leaned back in his chair. It was all so long ago. Then why did he feel as if he had been there? He was completely puzzled about his strong feelings concerning the death of the Texians. The front door opened and closed; then he heard his mother's brisk footsteps coming toward him.

"Benny, studying already? I am surprised!"

"No, not really. It's just that we went to La

Bahía today, you know, and I was checking up on a couple of things. Ray's coming over to study tonight. We have a test on Fannin and his men tomorrow."

"Well, good for you. I've been a little worried about your attitude toward Mr. Pruitt and that class. Everything seems to be better now, and I'm glad."

Benny closed the book he had been examining. "Didn't you once tell me that some of our relatives lived at La Bahía way back then?" But she hadn't heard him. He followed her into the kitchen where she put the groceries away and started supper. She left one small bag on the kitchen bar.

"What's that?" he asked idly.

"Just some stuff that was in the church rummage sale to be held on Saturday. We always get a chance to buy what we want before the sale starts. That's where I was all afternoon, sorting and pricing rummage."

"Who from our family lived at La Bahía?" Benny asked again, "and was it during the massacre, do you think?"

"Let's see. Your father's ancestor Mario Benito Cantú lived there in 1836, and there have been Cantús here in Goliad ever since. Each generation has had a Mario or a Benito, like you. I'd be happy to share all my genealogical information about our family with you. I never thought you'd be interested."

He really didn't want to get her started on genealogy. "I'm not, really," he said. "Just wondered." He pulled the paper bag with rummage toward himself. "I better check this out."

Reaching into the bag he withdrew a small oil painting, then a bud vase, but there was one more thing in the bottom wrapped in tissue paper. He pulled it out.

"What is this?"

"Look at it. It's a small pewter statue. I thought it was cute. Put it on the shelf of knickknacks in the living room."

He unwrapped the paper and set the tiny dog on the counter. The dog's ears stood erect, the little nose sniffed in the air, and the curly tail almost seemed to wag.

"Why does this thing look familiar to me?"

"Vera Thigpen, Ray's mom, donated it. I'm sure you've seen it many times over at Ray's house."

He looked at it for a moment, thinking. "Oh, sure. He's nice. Could I keep him in my room?"

"If you like. Now, would you rather have spaghetti or meat loaf for supper?"

"I don't care," he answered absently, and he carried the small figure into his bedroom and set it on top of his bookcase headboard. He stood beside the bed and gazed at the dog.

"You're mine now," he said. "I think I'll call you—Sparky. No, Paco. Yeah, Paco fits you just right." Then he hurried to change his clothes so that he could ride Rusty before supper.

Afterword

Looking Back on the Fannin Massacre

Although the name Edward (Taylor) Wingate is inscribed on the Fannin Memorial Monument in the list of those killed in the Massacre on March 27, 1836, at La Bahía, (now Goliad) Texas, he survived. Wingate's descendants spent many years tracing their ancestor and finally proved in court that the soldier did not die then but survived to fight again in the Texas War of Independence. He is counted as having fought in the Battle of Monterrey and other engagements. His second wife Eliza J. Wingate received a widow's pension when he died.

When the Texians were marched out of Fort Defiance (called La Bahía except during the Texas Revolution) and shot, Wingate escaped by diving into the San Antonio River. He was shot in the hip by Mexican soldiers. A kind Mexican family found him and nursed him back to health.

Like most of the 420 Texians in La Bahía, he was not from Texas. He had been born in North Carolina in 1802. Among the group fewer than twenty-five men were actually from Texas. Men who volunteered to fight in this war were lured by the offer of free land and, of course, the promise of adventure.

In December, 1868, Wingate died of pneumonia at the age of sixty-six with the musket ball still in his hip. More than 100 years later, his remains were reinterred in Fort Sam Houston National Cemetery, San Antonio, Texas, in 1960, with full military honors.

Wingate was typical of the adventurous type of volunteer who signed on to fight with Colonel James Walker Fannin. Like soldiers of fortune, these Texians, as they called themselves, were actively looking for a fight. The small contingents of men who were sent on various assignments such as helping the settlers in Refugio were really looking for opportunities to tangle with the Mexican forces. This led them into skirmishes they could not win since they were almost invariably outnumbered, ill equipped, and frequently outgunned.

Colonel Fannin exemplified this type of adventurer and may also have been flawed by the inability to make a firm decision when necessary. Communication was difficult in those days, and delays were sometimes fatal. Several times while he and about 400 Texians were in Fort Defiance, he hesitated too long and ultimately lost his own life and, according to the best sources, the lives of 342 brave soldiers. To be fair to his memory, it must be noted that the choices offered would probably have caused their deaths anyway.

This dark chapter in Texas history began in February of 1836 when Travis and about 150 men were trapped in the Alamo by General Santa Ana's almost 6000 soldiers. Travis sent frantic word to Fannin at La Bahía and to the Texians in Gonzalez to come to his aid. Thirty men from Gonzalez managed to get through to the Alamo. The Texians at La Bahía also tried to go to the aid of the Alamo on February 26, but their old, overworked wagons broke down. They had no food except beef jerky. They also faced a walk of 100 miles to the Alamo at San Antonio de Bexar, so they gave up and returned to Fort Defiance. They probably would have gone to their deaths if they had continued.

Although General Sam Houston ordered Fannin and the troops in Gonzalez to aid those in the Alamo, *the orders were not received until almost a week after the Alamo fell.*

By then, Fannin had released several groups on rescue missions around La Bahía and nearby Refugio. He felt that he must await their return before trying again to go to the aid of the Alamo. Although as far back as January, General Houston had warned Fannin not to send out small parties when the Mexicans were so near, Fannin seemed to have scoffed at the Mexicans' fighting abilities. It was a significant mistake and probably played a large part in his decision making.

The problem was that his men were more interested in fighting the Mexicans than in rescuing settlers. His troops were spoiling for a fight, and thus, did not return from their rescue missions speedily.

Fannin depended on them to tell him where the Mexicans were, but the men he had allowed to go were busy fighting. Without these intelligence sources, he was unable to plan.

On March 6, the Alamo fell and brought an end to the 182 Texians trapped there. The news of its fall did not reach Fannin until a week later on either March 13 or 14. General Sam Houston's order to Fannin to blow up Fort Defiance and retreat to Victoria arrived that day also.

Still Fannin delayed.

On March 19, the approximately 400 men at Fort Defiance finally began their retreat as ordered. They got only about nine miles, close to Coleto Creek. There, out in the open without food or water, their fate was sealed. General Urrea surrounded them and began killing and wounding Texians. The next day, Fannin sent a white flag of surrender to the Mexican forces at midday. By doing that, he hoped to be able to save his wounded men. He himself had been shot in the thigh.

The terms of the surrender have been in question ever since that day over 161 years ago. History offers the theory that although one copy was in Spanish, the other in English, the documents were not identical. Either that or the document Fannin signed was in Spanish and had been misinterpreted to him.

Fannin believed that he and his men would be treated like prisoners of war and although they would have to give up their weapons and promise not to fight in the Texas Revolution any more, they would be sent home.

But Urrea claimed that the Texians understood they had made an unconditional surrender and were subject to their captor's decision about their fate. The Mexicans called the Texians "pirates" and felt their fate should be similar to that of marauders on the high seas. Urrea did, however, offer to recommend to Santa Ana (spelled *Anna* in today's history books) that Fannin and his men should be spared execution. He claimed that he did so, and he may have.

Unfortunately, when Santa Ana's order of execution went to Urrea, he had moved on. The order was passed down to Colonel Juan Portilla who had been left in charge of the American prisoners in La Bahía. He was to march them out and kill them all, even the wounded. Thus, on Palm Sunday, March 27, 1836, 342 Texians were massacred and their bodies burned. About twenty-eight escaped: the doctors, who had treated the wounded Mexicans; the men captured without weapons who had been with Col. Miller at Copano; and a few secretly rescued by Señora Alavéz, known as "The Angel of Goliad."

Santa Ana's prime motive was to keep Texas as part of Mexico the way it had been. He was an advocate of a strong central government and intended to hold the country together no matter what. In the process, however, he became a tyrant both to the Mexican peasants and to the Texians.

On April 21, a little more than three weeks after

the La Bahía Massacre, it is not too surprising that the enraged Texian forces, numbering only 800, managed to overcome Santa Ana's 1500-1600 soldiers at San Jacinto to end the war. Their battle cries were "Remember the Alamo! Remember Goliad!"

Bibliography

Aikman, Lonnelle. *Nature's Healing Arts: From Folk Medicine to Modern Drugs*. The National Geographic Society, 1977.

Barnard, J.H. *Dr. J.H. Barnard's Journal* from December, 1835, to March 27, 1836, Giving an Account of Fannin Massacre. Edited by J.A. White, editor/owner of the *Goliad Advance* in 1912. Reproduced by Cyrus Milam White, March, 1965. Reproduced by the J.A. White family in June, 1988.

Buchman, Dian Dincin. *Herbal Medicine: The Natural Way to Stay Well*. London: Tiger Books International, 1979. Reprint. Random House, 1991.

Flynn, Jean. *Remember Goliad: James W. Fannin*. Austin: Eakin Press, 1984.

Grimes, Roy. *Goliad: 130 Years After*. Victoria, Texas: Victoria Advocate, 1966.

Grimes, Roy, editor. *300 Years in Victoria County*.

Victoria, Texas: *Victoria Advocate* Publishing Co., 1968. Reprint. Austin: Nortex Press, a division of Eakin Press, 1985.

Guthrie, Keith. *Texas' Forgotten Ports*. Austin: Eakin Press, 1988.

Meyer, Joseph. *The Herbalist*. 1918. Reprint. Glenwood, Illinois: Clarence Meyer, Meyerbooks, 1976.

Moore, Michel. *Los Remedios: Traditional Herbal Remedies of the Southwest*. Santa Fe, New Mexico: Red Crane Books, 1990.

Roell, Craig H. *Remember Goliad! A History of La Bahía*. Austin: Texas State Historical Association, 1994.

Torres, Eliseo. *Green Medicine: Traditional Mexican-American Herbal Remedies*. Kingsville, Texas: Nieves Press, 1992.

_____. *The Folk Healer: The Nexucab-American Tradition of Curanderismo*. Kingsville, Texas: Nieves Press, 1992.

Wharton, Clarence. *Remember Goliad! Texas, March 27, 1836*. 1931. Reprint. Glorieta, New Mexico: Rio Grande Press, Inc., 1968. [Copy acquired from

International Bookfinders, California.]

White, Nell. *Goliad in the Texas Revolution*. Master's thesis, University of Houston, May, 1941. 1988 printing by Nell White Hargreaves.

Acknowledgments to Pam Wingate, Rayburn Elementary Librarian; La Bahía Museum Director Newton M. Warzecha; Eugene Jacobs of Goliad and Austin, Texas, and the Wingate family of Texas.

Ms. Marvin stands before the flag mentioned on page 76.

About the Author

Native Texan Isabel Ridout Marvin lived in Goliad during her high school years. An English, Spanish, and journalism teacher, she now lives in Minnesota but spends winters in McAllen, Texas.

She is the author of many articles, short stories, and novels including the popular *Shipwrecked on Padre Island* published by Hendrick-Long.